HOW TO BULLSH*T YOUR WAY TO NUMBER 1:

AN UNORTHODOX GUIDE TO 21ST CENTURY SUCCESS FROM THE WORLD'S #1 FAKE RESTAURATEUR AND PARIS FASHION WEEK'S #1 FAKE DESIGNER

Oobah Butler

Published in 2019 by Oobah Butler
26 Worth Grove
Walworth, London, SE172HN

Printed in the United States of America
First Issue Print: **#1 out of 20,000**

Cover design by Tristan Cross

ISBN: 9781513643656

To Dean Noroozi (the man who rented me the Shed), Victoria and Paul Butler, Chris Tarrant and Vanessa Swanson

CONTENTS

PROLOGUE TO PROLOGUE

Hi, I'm Oobah Butler, and here's how bullshit changed my life.

In 2017, I embarked on the stupidest and most successful prank of my career: turn the backyard shed I lived in at the time into the Number 1-rated restaurant in London, then invite strangers to come and dine in my garden. The challenge was: would anyone know it wasn't real? Or would they assume this was the workings of a mad idiot and shop me to the police?

Well, long story short: I wasn't arrested. In fact, I've become the opposite of arrested: after the video explaining what I did went viral (41.4 million views to date), I've become more successful than I've ever been, after appearing on the UK's most-watched morning TV show Good Morning Britain, being written about in the Washington Post and profiled in Forbes, being debated in Singaporean parliament, being the subject of an hour-long documentary on Japanese TV. In the year since the video came out, I've gone viral again, (twice), and my life is now spent jetting around the globe, either talking at conferences to tell other people the secrets of my success (I've spoken in Bangladesh, Sweden, Germany, San Francisco) or filming my first original TV series (which I can't tell you about, but you're going to love). I'm richer than ever, people ask me to teach them the ways of my success more than ever, and crucially I no longer live in a shed. And how did I do it?

Well, hard work, a fair about of luck, lots of caffeine and a fair amount of persistence.

But also, very crucially:

A whole load of bullshit.

PROLOGUE

The backyard shed I was living in was never meant to be the number one-rated restaurant in London.

Backyard sheds, in general, are not supposed to be restaurants. Maybe you keep a shovel in yours, or one of those really long garden hoses. Maybe you keep the remains of cans of paint in the exact same colour as your hallway, in case you ever need to touch up the paintwork (you are never going to touch up the paintwork). Maybe your shed is home to a mass of spiders and a bike you told yourself you were going to ride to work this week but didn't. It doesn't matter what is in your shed, because nobody looks in there, least of all you. Last time you tried to open the door you heard that dreadful sound of three things collapsing at once – like when you stack plates in a cupboard and hear them all shuffle behind the closed door – and thought: "Not my problem." You went inside and put the TV on. You forgot your shed even existed at all.

My shed wasn't my shed in the traditional sense, it was my home. Or, rather, it wasn't even my shed: it was someone else's shed that I rented from them for £800 a month and lived in with my girlfriend. In the back of the garden of a house in south-east London, for two years, I lived in a shed-shaped box with a faulty shower, a washing machine that occasionally got confused about the ideal direction of the sewage pump (I maintain that the ideal direction is out. The washing machine had other ideas.) and, yes, a normal shed's worth of spiders.

But then, in 2017, I had an idea. And that turned into another idea. And with a lot of hard work – and a whole lot of bullshit – I managed to turn that idea, and my rented shed, into something else entirely.

I managed to turn it into success.

I managed to turn it into a business.

I managed to turn it into a job.

I managed to turn it into fame.

I managed to turn my shed into the best-rated restaurant in London.

And what I learned along the way can help you do it too. You don't have to go and live in a shed – I would honestly say it is preferable if you didn't – but you have to have a 'shed mindset'. You have to have a metaphorical shed – a box full of spiders you want to turn into gold – and the drive to do it. In 11 months, I went from living in a shed to appearing on primetime TV, and less than two years later I am flying around the world giving speeches to CEOs, company presidents, award-winning thinkers and million-aires, telling them all about that time my washing machine made a horrible clunking noise and started filling with human shit.

It does not matter if your washing machine is full of shit if your heart is still pure.

Over those 11 months, I developed a way of thinking that I have used again and again – and taught to many others – that can make even the strangest idea a huge success.

I overcame obstacles, both physical and mental, and perse-vered to make something that has changed my life wholly for the better.

I battled naysayers and negativity and proved my many doubters wrong.

I got that washing machine fixed, at great personal cost to myself.

And I developed a mental toolkit that can be taught, used, and repeated, over and over, to take that tiny spark of an idea you have – that little glimmer of gold in your boxful of spiders – and turn it into something big, and loud, and real.

It doesn't matter what you want to achieve, or how badly you want it: if you attempt to do a job with the wrong tools in your hands, you're never going to finish it.

You wouldn't try to hammer a nail into a wall with a three-day old baguette, would you? You wouldn't try to cross a lake on a raft made of straw. You wouldn't try to make your clothes clean in a large metal box filled with liquefied shit.

In this book, I will give you the tools to make any idea of yours real, solid, and successful.

I turned my shed into the number one-rated restaurant in London. Think what I can teach you to do.

IDENTIFY YOUR 'SHED'

We're going to go on a journey together that starts at rock bottom, somehow manages to go a little deeper to a place far beneath rock bottom, and then ascends high above both your and my expectations. We have to do this because that's how I did this. Maybe you can skip a few steps – maybe you can start from a place that's medium-bottom, or even just 'somewhere quite normal' – but I'm going to tell you how I started low and went lower, because it's crucial to my (and your) eventual success.

I'm going to need you to identify your 'shed'.

In 2015, I moved into a shed. I admit this isn't normal. It had heating, and electricity, and a bed in it – all the things you most likely have in your house or flat! – but, from the outside, it was definitely a shed. The first day we moved in, I put my foot through the damp wooden deck just outside the shed, and from then on we constantly had a foot-shaped hole directly outside our front door. A month after that a pregnant fox got in through the foot-shaped-hole and nestled deep under the foundations of the shed, where she gave birth to four beautiful, loud, red little cubs. Have you ever heard the sound a fox makes when it's a frolicking cub? It's high, and deranged, and awful. They would start up at 3 a.m. and not stop until the sun started to creep through our curtains. Me, to my girlfriend, during The Spring When The Foxes Came, as we came to know it: "Hey, can you hear those foxes?" Her, to me, with that quiet anger you only get when you are really in trouble: "... yes, Oobah."

This lesson isn't going to be vital for our journey, but it's a useful one to know anyway:

Foxes have no respect for the human concept of time.

The shed wasn't always my rock bottom. I first moved to London the year before, and lived in a flatshare with a handful of other people. Eventually I realized that I needed my own space but couldn't afford the fancy London living that comes with it. Living in a shed in someone's garden ticked a lot of the boxes: I could live with my girlfriend so we could split the rent and bills, we weren't constantly pestered by the comings and goings of our housemates (unless you count baby foxes, but seeing as they didn't contribute to the rent, I didn't), and I only had to plan a showering schedule around one other person. For a summer, shed life was good; we were alone in a lush verdant garden, we came and went as we pleased, and we had a good life (read: there were three nice brunch spots within walking distance) in one of London's most sought-after neighborhoods. I was 24 years old. When you're 24 years old, you can live with some foxes in a shed. You can basically sleep in an on-fire trashcan when you're 24.

But over time, shed-life started to wear, and the available non-shed options seemed less viable than toughing it out in the back of someone else's garden. Upgrading to a one-bed flat somewhere would drastically spike our rent, and my salary couldn't stretch to accommodate the increase. Finding somewhere that would just about suit our budget would yank us even further out of London, making travelling and commuting and socializing even harder. We were at an impasse: the shed had been our home for two years, but we had outgrown the novelty of it, while the city's rental market had a growth spurt around us. What once felt like a very freeing living situation suddenly felt more like we'd trapped ourselves in a strange, shed-shaped prison.

At this point, I got made redundant from my main source of income, which was writing copy for a coupon code website. Suddenly, the pipe dream of moving out of the shed and into a house with walls and no foxes got even more distant. We'd been in London together four years. It seemed like we were travelling backwards, not forwards. Around this time the washing machine did the filling-itself-with-shit thing I talked about earlier. At this point, I realised this: **living in the shed was my rock bottom.**

It didn't feel like it at the time, but this was a good realization to have.

Once you know how low you can get and still keep going, everything from there is improvement.

And, crucially, you find a new appreciation for everything that's better than your rock bottom. If I won $5 on the lottery that week? That would have felt like a huge victory. If I got a low-paying job that covered my rent? That would have felt gigantic.

The fact that I managed to turn this situation into the position I'm sitting in now – sharing my hard-learned wisdom, teaching you the Tao of Bullshit – feels, when contrasted to the lowest point of my life, living in the shed, exhilarating. Take stock of where you are, right now. Even if you're in a good place, I promise you, we're going to go bigger. And every step up and away from it is going to feel amazing.

WHY YOU'RE FULL OF BULLSHIT

It's important to caveat this with the following: Hey, maybe you're not full of bullshit. I'm sure you're a nice person! I'm sure you're great, and not full of bullshit at all. But I think it's important, before any journey that involves taking an idea and making it a success, to interrogate why you haven't done it already. Like: why are you reading this book about making it to #1? Why aren't you just Number 1 already?

You're not Number 1 yet because you haven't let yourself be Number 1.

So maybe you're not full of bullshit, but maybe the Excuse Center in your brain is. You know the one, the one that kicks into gear every time a friend texts you on a rainy Saturday morning to remind you that you have plans; you'd agreed to go with them to that flower arranging workshop, you remember, the one they said they'd always like to go to and the one that you, two glasses of wine down and a fortnight ago, said was a great idea. This is an impression of you, making those plans:

"I will absolutely be there. Oh my god." [really long period where you go through the Calendar app on your phone with a single finger extended to them to "shush" while you confirm you have no plans on that day] "I'm totally free that day. I'm putting you in my calendar right now. Oh my god." [Pause while you drink more wine] "Flowers!"

So now it's Saturday morning and you're sitting in sweatpants on your sofa and your phone blips and it's your friend going: 'Still on for later?' Is there a more dreadful text to receive in the English-speaking world than 'Still on for later?' I think I'd honestly rather get 'HPV results inconclusive, please call us'. 'Are you the family of [your mother's entire name]?' is better than 'Still on for later?'. 'Still on for later?' says: I know you forgot but you said you wouldn't. You're stuck.

This is where the Bullshit Cortex in your brain goes into overdrive. Weigh how much you Really Don't Want To Do This against The Negative Social Consequences Of Not Doing This. You're really very comfy on the sofa. It's raining outside and your good autumnal gear is hanging on the laundry rack to dry, still wet. You planned this Saturday! You did laundry! You were going to enjoy a day doing domestic chores! You don't even like flowers! Here's what you do: you compose a really long text saying "I'm so sorry", throw in some lie about...maybe you're feeling ill? No; someone in your family is feeling ill. Hold on: you have to leave the city right now and it's a really short notice thing, I'm so sorry. Press send. Your friend understands, but they know that you are lying. Snuggle up on that sofa, baby. Maybe have a little nap this afternoon. You earned it.

It feels good, yes, but this is your Bullshit Cortex acting like a handbrake stopping you from achieving things. Day-to-day, it's fine, but it's also always there, ticking along in the background, making excuses for you to not do things. 'Shall we run for that bus?' you ask the Bullshit Cortex, and the Bullshit Cortex whispers, 'Running for buses is for losers. Catch the next one.' You're 15 minutes late for work. Or, 'Should we text that cool friend who we're always slightly too intimidated to text and see what they're up to, because they're so cool and sort of intimidating in a way that you treat the friendship between you as this very delicate thing, like a bowl made of fine glass, that could break and shatter at any time if you handle it too brutally?' and the Bullshit Cortex in your brain goes, 'No, come on. They won't text back. Order a pizza and have an early night.' That cool friend tried heroin that evening! That could have been you! What a story that would have been! You missed out, all because of your Bullshit Cortex!

And, crucially, your Bullshit Cortex is always there telling you to stop being so ambitious. 'Should I run with that idea we have and try and turn it into a business?' you ask your Bullshit Cortex, and it goes into overdrive: 'Businesses are expensive. You'd need a loan. You'd need a website, and you don't know how to make websites! You don't know anything about business. You've never completed an idea before. You don't—'

If I had listened to my Bullshit Cortex, I would never have made a restaurant out of my shed. The Bullshit Cortex is the voice that is always telling you 'no'. Sometimes it is looking out for you. Often it is protecting you. But sometimes it is smothering you.

You need to learn to cast off the yoke of your own bullshit.

BUILD YOUR TOOLBOX

This isn't a hard task. The greatest enemy of the Bullshit Cortex is structured thinking. Take a pen (a good one, not some shitty ballpoint pen. You know you don't enjoy writing with those, but you do like making fat marks with a Sharpie, so get one), get a notebook (you have at least three unopened notebooks that are very cute and that you keep buying in shops, twice yearly, for 'projects' that you never get around to doing. I know this because I do too. Get one of them.) and sit down with no phone, no distractions, maybe a little music and a glass of water, but that's all I'm letting you have. Write down the words 'BULLSHIT CORTEX' at the top of the page. Confront your demon.

BULLSHIT CORTEX

Then, underneath it, write your idea. For the purposes of this exercise, our idea is...what if corn flakes were chocolate-flavoured?

BULLSHIT CORTEX

WHAT IF CORN FLAKES WERE CHOCOLATE-FLAVOURED?

Then, to overwhelm the B.C. with logic, you just need to write down the pros and the cons in a list format. Yes, I know this may seem simple. The Bullshit Cortex is already there to provide the CONs for you. But if you can sit and think of a PRO to counter every CON, then the voice of doubt has been defeated. You just need to reason with it, and not take the first 'no' you get (or invent yourself) as the ultimate answer. Look:

BULLSHIT CORTEX

WHAT IF CORN FLAKES WERE CHOCOLATE-FLAVOURED?

PRO	CON
They could be called 'Choccies'	Necessarily, they would not longer be healthy. Cornflakes are an adult cereal targeted at people who, like, care about their cholesterol and shit. Selling chocolate-flavour to them, instead of children, is a tough ask.

Corn flakes were originally designed to be a cereal so boring they could actually diminish horniness in men and young adolescents, causing them to masturbate less, and I truly think chocolate-flavoured Corn flakes would have the exact inverse effect and it would be chaos.

They would taste, I'm pretty sure, absolutely hauntingly terrible once they got even remotely soggy.

OK, listen, yes: in this case, the Bullshit Cortex was right, although I maintain that 'Choccies' is a great name for a cereal and would make for some astonishing advertising jingles. But sometimes it's still good to write it down, see it in black and white, interrogate it from every angle, and come out with a firm yes or no. Is your idea a winner? Sometimes, it's not going to be. Sometimes, it absolutely is. But you're only going to know that once you stop listening to the big flashing NO in your head, kick the Bullshit Cortex in the nuts (in this analogy the Bullshit Cortex is anthropomorphized. In the film it could be played by someone ornery and squat, like Joe Pesci), and figure it out for yourself.

So maybe you don't live in a shed with no direction and a washing machine full of shit. But perhaps you live in a metaphorical shed (your mind) and you're a hostage to your Bullshit Cortex (also your mind). We need to get you out of there, stat.

PICK YOURSELF UP, DICKHEAD!

The Shed started out as a joke. One of my first writing jobs, when I first moved to London, was doing fake TripAdvisor reviews – businesses would pay around £10 a review for you to log on to their TripAdvisor or Google Review pages and leave something gushing but realistic, a four- or five-star review of their services, to improve their overall score. Was this extremely dodgy? Yes. Is it technically immoral? I mean...yes. Did it pay my rent for a good year because, once you get yourself going, you can actually make quite a decent hourly rate out of it? Also yes. I have had a complicated relationship with the website – and the nature of peer-reviewed restaurant ratings (never trust them) – ever since.

So, The Shed initially started out as a project to push the concept of unethical and false TripAdvisor reviews to the logical conclusion: it was never meant to ever serve food. London restaurants are slaves to these rankings; they do their best to offer the best service, the best and most consistent foods, the most seasonally reworked menus, the greatest dining experiences, just to fight their ways to the top of it. Being at the top of the TripAdvisor rating list is a lucrative business; you get more tourists reserving tables at your restaurants and more calls every day to reserve tables. The idea that came to me was this: could me and, say, 30 of my friends get a restaurant that didn't exist to the top of London's TripAdvisor rating list without frying a single egg?

Yes.

Here was the plan to get to the top:

THE PLAN TO GET TO THE TOP

1.   I put a Facebook message out (and sent a few texts, and a

reply-all email thread that ended up getting a bit out of hand) asking for help. I'm a weird guy who typically operates at quite a weird frequency, so when I asked the people I know, 'Hey, could you review the shed I live in and call a home and say it's the best restaurant you've ever been to?' they weren't surprised. The first job was to recruit participants. It didn't take as many as you'd think.

2. We needed consistency: it wouldn't be convincing if one reviewer said, 'This is the best vegan restaurant I've ever been to!' and another said 'the steak was perfectly medium-rare'. I introduced three golden rules to all reviewers: the restaurant was al fresco dining (I mean...it's a shed), the experience was very unique, and the menu was set, not by meat or fish, starters or mains, but by 'mood'. You could choose 'Romantic', for example, or 'Slightly Angry'. 'Horny' was a bestselling dish. This gave The Shed an evocative feeling: more like a dining experience than a two-mains-and-a-bottle-of-wine-for-two pasta and pizza place.

3. Third, I had to set up a TripAdvisor page for my Shed. This took me buying a £10 trap phone from my local store. These phones are normally favoured by people who need a quick, untraceable, unregistered phone number, so...drug dealers. I cannot go to that newsagent anymore because he keeps looking at me like he wants to buy ketamine. I registered my restaurant on TripAdvisor under that number. We also set up a rudimentary website and, with my photographer friend Chris, took some food photos. One was a dishwasher detergent tablet covered in honey. Another was a blob of foam shaving cream scattered with pepper. In the right light, anything can look like food. I still refused to fry even a single egg.

4. Wait for the reviews to roll in. Thankfully, not everyone got on board with this plan right away, which meant the reviews were posted periodically; on the first day we got five or six, a couple more the next day, then it trailed off. Over the

course of a few months, we slowly climbed the rankings, me reminding people now and again to log on and post a review. The benefit to this timing was that the reviewing pattern looked organic. It tricked TripAdvisor's supposedly stringent anti-doping algorithms. Slowly, we climbed, breaking into the top 1,000 restaurants in London, then the top 500. I was doing other projects at the time, but the more success I had pushing The Shed to Number 1, the more obsessed I got. The Shed was ranked 237th in London, then close to the top 100 restaurants in the city. A big push one evening broke us into the top 87. It delighted me to think of all those thousand of restaurants out there, in London – pushing out orders, smiling at staff, divvying out tips, frying eggs, washing the kitchen, paying overheads – while I was just here, cackling at home, topless in my shed, slowly outranking them in the listings. Inch-by-inch, I crept towards the top of the list.

At this point I realised I didn't have a plan.

There's a moment in Seinfeld, the greatest sitcom ever made, where George finally loses his patience with Kramer after he signs up for an adult fantasy camp. "Kramer goes to a fantasy camp?" he rages. "His whole life is a fantasy camp. People should plunk down two-thousand dollars to live like him for a week. Do nothing, fall ass-backwards into money, mooch food off your neighbors, and have sex without dating. That's a fantasy camp!" That quote has always stuck with me, because I think everyone has a Kramer in their life; someone who, without any visible effort, like a swan moving gracefully across a lake without paddling their legs, seems to float from one life achievement to another. Think about your friend group right now. If you do not have a Kramer, you are the Kramer. With The Shed, I'd Kramered myself. I'd fallen ass-backwards into a good idea while trying to annoy TripAdvisor for no reason, and now I didn't know what to do with it.

THE THEORY OF 'SO WHAT'?

Why had I done this? I think that's the first question I had to ask myself and, as we go on this bullshit journey together, you'll have to ask yourself too: why am I doing what I'm doing? To what end is this? I'd cracked my shed into the Top 100 on the TripAdvisor rankings with no particular reason in mind. What was I doing here?

Before The Shed turned into the big idea it eventually became, it was, essentially, a prank that got out of hand. A lot of my ideas start like this (as you'll come to understand later) and I maintain that doing something just for the hell of it is a good way of starting any creative idea. You see where it goes, how it grows and spreads organically, what it becomes without your direct guidance. The Shed had cracked the Top 100, but what was this for? A lot of the friends I'd recruited to help me power it up the list where asking me this. Why? What for? What's the endgame?

And I thought about it for a while, and then I realised. Yes, I had sort of done this for no reason. And **So What?**

A lot of human behaviour can be explained. You can go deep into the brains – all the synapses and little electrical spurts – and you can go bigger picture, to cortexes and human psychology, and you can go to the past an examine the lizard brain, and you can go through academia and explain emotions, and love, and interactions with friends, and why we get jealous, and why we cry at *The Notebook*. But there's also a grey area of human behaviour that is just impulse. You ever just find yourself, like, buying a share-sized Snickers® and gobbling it alone at a bus stop? You ever wander into a shop you know you're not going to buy anything in and just soothe yourself for 15 minutes by picking up and handling expensive bowls? Sometimes you do things just for the hell of it. You don't explain it with logic, or go into it knowing what the net goal is, or how this thing you're doing is important to you on your journey.

You just do it...because. You just do it because...**So What?**

My theory is: you get one **So What** a day, and one, big **So What** a month. Don't feel like responding to that urgent e-mail today? So What. Got salad in the fridge but want to order fancy take-out for dinner? So What. So what can be big or small, but fundamentally it's a way of forgiving yourself into behaving the way you want to behave without the cold guilty cowl of logic hanging over everything you do.

Say you want to start a business taking ornate Victorian-style photographs of people's pets, as a fun keepsake (I'm going to tell you now, this is a weak to very-weak business proposal, and that's not just the Bullshit Cortex speaking, this is objectively a bad idea). It's your passion, it's what you want to do. A lot of people are going to question you on this. They'll ask, 'Why? What is the market for these photos? Who in their right mind would pay for these? On what basis do you think there is mass demand for black-and-white photographs of haunted-looking dogs wearing top hats and waist-coats?' And when people come to you with those questions, hit them with a big **So What.** It's not spectacular and it's not clever. But it is your idea, and you want to do it. So **So What** to everybody else.

Yeah, I turned my shed-house into a Top 100-rated London restaurant. So What?

REALITY BITES

The first time the phone rang, I panicked.

The drug dealer phone I'd had clonking around in my rucksack for weeks finally rang. The battery on these things, by the way, is astounding. They really are a practical device for taking multiple drug requests every night, or perfect for smuggling into prison up your ass. Until now, I'd never considered that it would ever ring; I'd only bought it because the TripAdvisor page required a phone number to register. But now it was ringing – bzz, bzz, moving across my coffee table like an angry insect – and I picked it up and looked at it. UNKNOWN NUMBER. Was I...doing...this?

"H–hello?"

"Hello, is that The Shed at Dulwich?"

I paused. I'd been working on a few other projects in recent weeks – I'd sort of forgotten about asking all my friends to review the shed I lived in and say it was a fabulous restaurant.

"Yes?"

"I was wondering if you had a table for two available? For this Saturday?"

The voice on the phone was like a lot of voices that live around the Dulwich area: slightly posh, a little accentless, someone who went to university in the late nineties and bought a house before the recession hit, who has a good income to play with and likes to go out to eat at fascinating new restaurant ventures, who pays the babysitter good money to look after their two perfect, cherub-like children to come and eat my...what? A dishwasher tablet covered in honey?

"I'm so sorry, we're fully booked this weekend." My face cringed in on itself. "We, uh, have a six-week waiting list."

"Oh," the voice said. "I understand. Thanks for letting me know." They clicked off and hung up. I stared at the phone. People wanted to come and eat at my restaurant based on a fantasy. Because of my rules, and my plan, someone in one of the grand houses that sat surrounding my shed wanted to spend their Saturday night outside, eating a meal called 'Horny', which included whatever I wanted to serve to them.

Suddenly, I was Kramer. I'd fallen ass-backwards into something. And it felt electrifying.

TOOLKIT

Sometimes ideas creep up on you. At this point – topless, alone in my shedroom (bed + shed = shedroom), staring at my trap phone, I looked, to all the world, like a man without a clue. But an idea had just fallen into my lap, and I needed to do something with it. This was no longer about living in a shed, a mere slave to my Bullshit Cortex. This was something else. **You know a good idea when it wriggles and dances inside of you, and this was mine.** I'd tricked a potential paying customer into thinking my restaurant was real, and now it was time to make it something more.

IT TAKES A VILLAGE TO CREATE SOME BULLSHIT

It's hard to make things happen on your own. I couldn't have made my Shed the 87th best restaurant in London with just me writing the reviews. I'd needed my friends, and I'd needed the Plan, and I now needed them on board with the idea. Knowing I was so high up the TripAdvisor list that people would call me to ask about it gave me the impetus I needed. To climb up to the top ten, or even the dizzying heights of #1, I needed everyone to put in a double-shift. **I needed all hands on deck.**

Social media is obviously the worst thing to happen to the human brain since...no, I'm pretty sure we've never created anything quite so dangerous for our psyche than that (maybe...torture? maybe...LSD?). The point is, in rare instances when you're not arguing with people over the correct way to pronounce 'scone' or something similarly pointless, its power can be harnessed for good. Think the Arab Spring, but instead of overturning a corrupt government by way of people power, we were trying to pull the pants of TripAdvisor down and make people come to my shed for a microwaved meal.

I realised I needed to make my fantasy a reality. I was given an opportunity, and I was going to take it. For one night only, I was going to be the top-rated restaurant in London. But I couldn't do it on my own.

Sometimes you need people with skills: eventually, I was going to need a **chef**, a talented and convincing **waitress**, and a **man who knew how to hold chickens by the legs.** But right now what I needed was people, sheer people. I needed numbers. I put the call out every way I could. Phone calls, e-mails, tweets, Facebook. I got friends to email their friends, get their mums and their mum-friends involved. The reviews started to pour in. With a sustained effort, over the course of only a few weeks, The Shed climbed. And climbed. And climbed again. Top 50, the calls to the drug dealer phone became daily. Top 25 and the phone rang three times an hour. In the Top 10 I started to run out of excuses. I was ignoring calls, getting passive-aggressive texts ("Are you ever open?"), a man even called from Italy and tried to book my shed to eat in on Christmas Day. And then, one night, when I'd travelled on a three-hour train back to Redditch to go and house-sit for my parents over the course of a sleepy autumn weekend, I logged on to TripAdvisor to check my ranking. **I was the number #1 rated restaurant in London.**

I yelled and yelled and yelled and yelled.

EXAMPLE

Listen, perhaps you're not trying to get your shed to become the #1 rated restaurant in London. I understand you might not have that urge. But at the early stages of your idea, you need to have as many people on your side – friends, family, vague acquaintances – as possible. You cannot make it happen on your own, so you should never be afraid of asking for help from people. Get people to rally around a cause by doing something that requires of them very little effort. It didn't cost my friends any money to get involved in this scheme; it barely cost them any time. It took five minutes of them doing a favour to me, and I was on my way.

OK, so say your idea is...you want to start a modeling agency for rabbits. Some rabbits are cute, sure, but a real rabbit – a commercially viable rabbit – you recognize that that's a hard thing to come by. You've made a shiny website and set up a dedicated trap phone line. You have two or three cute rabbits of your own. But you need more rabbits on your books. You need to find and **identify your town's hottest rabbits.**

Do your friends have rabbits? Do they have any family with rabbits? Could they put a call out on their Facebook, or email the people they know? Make a poster that can easily be shared that reads, 'Do You Have A Commercially Attractive Rabbit? Do You Want To Make Income From Your Rabbit, Which Is Otherwise Sitting At Home Doing Nothing? Have You Ever Considered Monetizing Your Rabbit? I Can Make It Happen.' Put your details at the bottom and wait for people to get in touch. **Everyone who owns a rabbit thinks their rabbit is the prettiest rabbit.**

It's a silly example maybe, but it illustrates a point. You can have the best idea in the world, but if you don't get people on board with it – if you don't spread your idea, the existence of it, if you don't make people aware, and if you don't get people talking – you're going to get nowhere. This is, possibly, the bullshittiest step of the entire operation: **speaking your idea into existence.** Bullshit hard enough and fluently enough and it becomes real. Tell enough people you're doing something enough times through enough mediums, and they'll eventually turn up to watch. Even if it's a quite strange rabbit fashion show that ends abruptly when someone's terrible dog arrives.

IT'S TIME TO GO PRO

Once I'd hit the #1 spot, I knew I was on to something, if for no other reason than that I was taking dozens of calls every day. I'd once accidentally left the phone at my friend's house for 24 hours. When I came back to retrieve it, I had 114 missed calls. I'd created buzz and hype without really ever setting out to do that, but one way or another, I had something in my hands worth focusing on.

It was time to make the idea a reality.

Like the chocolate cornflakes ('Choccies – The Corn Flake For Kids!'™) from our previous Toolkit section, not every idea makes it to this stage, and that's okay, but when you do hit upon an idea that has a momentum seemingly of its own, it's up to you to know when to turn it into something. I could have just left it there. I could have shut the phone off forever, shuttered the website, and known that I'd achieved something many actual restaurants never end up doing: I'd made it to the top spot. But I didn't: instead, I'd launched myself out of The Shed, and into a life of glamorous scheming.

I'd proved what I set out to do, so why didn't I stop there? **Because this bullshit had its own energy.**

It would have been easy for me not to do anything with this. In fact, arguably, it would have been the easiest path overall. That's the Bullshit Cortex way of doing things. Get yourself up to the starting line, then shrink away when the starting gun goes off. This is the point where, crucially, you have to take control: **your idea is a steam engine generating power, and it's up to you to decide where to make it go before it runs out of momentum.**

You could give up, and it could all fold, never to reach its shimmering final destination, just at the end of the horizon. Or, you could pull the rev the engine, put the work in, and make it something ever faster, and shinier, and better.

Long story short, I decided to turn my fake restaurant into a real restaurant.

MAKING BULLSHIT A REALITY

First things first, I had my location, which was the shed I lived in in someone else's backyard. I had a vague blueprint for the project, too. Thanks to the rules I'd set for my friends' TripAdvisor reviews, I'd already built the word-of-mouth idea of a restaurant as an experience rather than a fine-dining establishment. Nobody was going to turn up and expect haughty waiters and Michelin-starred food, because the reviews had already said they'd be eating outside, ordering according to 'mood', and that the entire eating experience was 'quirky.' After all, this is London, where you can get away with that sort of thing. (This was, it turns out, very serendipitous: I couldn't have made The Shed a reality without the accidental genius-stroke of telling my friends to review the restaurant as if it were quirky. The one takeaway lesson from this is: despite all your best intentions, **dumb luck is still going to be a part of everything you do**).

This still didn't mean I was restaurant-ready, though. I couldn't just take a few reservations for Friday night, put some chairs out, serve the patrons a big veggie casserole and wait for the money to roll in. **I'd built a brand monument, and now I needed to build an experience to match.**

I realized that it was important to enter into this knowing my limitations. I'm a master of bullshit, sure, but I can't bullshit my way through cooking a meal, balancing the fine-line scheduling and plate-spinning of a restaurant service, and making ten people dinner without breaking down and crying. I needed a chef to do all of that for me. On top of that, while I was operating the restaurant from within, pulling the strings, I needed a face of the shop. Specifically, I needed a waitress who not only knew the goal of

The Shed (to...erm...something-something TripAdvisor), but also had the confidence to override with sheer charisma diners' inevitable doubts about the place, and keep everything ticking without my needing to get involved. I also needed the logistical stuff like chairs, tables, outside heaters. I needed the boring things like food and ingredients that I could then cook into food. I needed, basically, an entire restaurants' worth of stuff, crammed into my shed where I'd already run out of space to put all my jeans. I was up against a hurdle, but what I crucially needed to do was this:

Recruit people, and recruit the right people.

This, I think, is where the whole idea could have so easily gone down in flames, and it's the turning point where a lot of young businesses and exciting ideas can go to shit. Once you've built a foundation of bullshit, you need to construct something on top of it, and the first few people you rope in to support your idea as it gains momentum are crucial. Listen, Facebook has 25,000 employees worldwide. You think it matters if they accidentally hire a lazy programmer, who keeps taking really long lunch breaks, turns up half an hour after everyone else, has a loudly bad attitude and for some reason disappears from his desk for 20 minutes every afternoon to go and put an old dollar bill into the vending machine to try and get a Baby Ruth to come out? No, it doesn't matter. Soon enough that guy will fail his performance review and be summarily hauled in front of Mark Zuckerberg to be executed in typical Facebook fashion, which is where Zuck stares at him in silence with those strange alien eyes of his until the guy's head and brain start bleeding.

But when Facebook first started out? Those first five, ten employees were everything. Everyone involved had to be absolutely on the same page, with the same drive and energy, the same passion for success, and the same will to make it happen. A lazy employee who keeps shouting, 'Margarita Time!' every afternoon is a luxury, and it's a luxury that small companies and tiny ideas can't afford to indulge. Once you get to the stage where you can indulge those kinds of luxuries, consider yourself to have made it.

I'm not saying The Shed was a Facebook-sized idea. I mean, for one, I haven't been hauled in front of Congress to explain it (yet), nor have I made a billion dollars from it. Your idea might not turn out to be Facebook-sized either. But small successful ideas have to adhere to the same formula as big successful ideas, which is as follows.

THE FORMULA TO SUCCESS

Right Idea, Right Time, Right People + Hard Work + Bullshit + Fair Amount of Luck But Let's Not Dwell On That = Success!

FINDING THE RIGHT PEOPLE

I found my chef at a party when I was really, really drunk. I was mentally in a different time zone – I'd just flown back home from New York, so I was still on Eastern Time, wildly out of whack with Greenwich Mean Time, and my eyes were rolling out of my head. My friend, Tom Gorton, who had heard about the project, introduced me to his friend, Joe, and he just got it. We all clicked, stayed up until 6 in the morning (easy for me, as my body was wired into that time. For them...not so much), and vowed to get in touch the day after. There, on New York time and eight or nine beers down, I was convinced I had found my man.

But here's the thing: as well as phone calls to the restaurant from customers, I'd started to get businesses getting in touch with The Shed too. I suppose this is the great con, the thing that made me realise bullshit is universal in every business you're in. Seeing me at the top of the TripAdvisor rankings, had led to PR companies wanting to represent me, ingredient stockists contacting me trying to get their wares placed in my restaurant (I got sent a box of loose leaf tea that I'm still working my way through because... who uses loose leaf tea? Come on, mate. Send me teabags and then we can talk.), and chefs and wait staff speculatively sending me their resumes hoping to work with or for me.

Thus, I came upon my first big compromise of the whole escapade.

MY FIRST BIG COMPROMISE OF THE WHOLE ESCAPADE

When I first decided to turn this idea from a big joke into a slightly bigger but more real joke, I was convinced that I would hire a chef and also waiters from these people who had emailed me their resumes. That, in my initial thinking, was the funniest and best way to do this. To hire an **actual chef** who had applied for an **actual job** at my shed, pair them up with **actual wait staff** who needed an evening's work, and go from there. I'd already sifted through a few resumes, and even had a phone interview with a very sweet lady who promised to cook up three-course Malaysian cuisine. Meeting Joe, woozily drunk and on the wrong timezone, was a random, off-plan deviation. **It wasn't part of my original vision.**

But for it to work, it had to be him. For one, he'd had a peep behind the curtain of my wild idea and he liked what he saw. He understood what I was doing and why, and he thought it was funny too. He was willing to give up a couple of days of his time (Joe is an actual chef, who plates and serves in a fancy London restaurant in the West End) to help my cause. I knew he'd do the job properly. We can take two vision-centric lessons from this:

1.   It's important to have people who see your vision on your team
2.   Prioritizing doing the job right rather than doing it by my original vision turned out to be the best decision I made.

On the night of, Joe was amazing. He made the kitchen his own domain, kept the food – which, let's face it, is the whole essence of the experience – pumping out of the kitchen, and honestly I've been to real restaurants where I've had to wait longer for my food. He was the right person for the job because he took food service by the scruff of the neck and made it his own. I needed someone who knew what they were doing, and got why we were doing it, and I found one. Though it would have been funny as part of my wider plan to have the Malaysian cuisine cooked by a stranger who thought she'd been hired by a real restaurant, getting Joe to do some frozen pasta bakes in the oven turned out to be the better decision on the night. **I had to learn to re-prioritize my focus when the situation called for it.**

TOOLKIT

Tempted as I am to say 'get exceedingly drunk three hours after an eight-hour, transatlantic flight and hire the first person who says "hello" to you', that's not exactly the most practical advice, especially if the two-day hangover that succeeded it was anything to go by. Take stock of everyone you know. Do they have skills that can help you make your idea a reality? Do they have areas of expertise that you can't possibly hope to learn in the time needed to do it? Take stock, also, of who **they** know. My friend Tom is an arts editor who knows practically everyone, and I think you have a friend like this too. Everyone does; someone who seems to attract experts in their fields into their friend group. I suppose the short version of this is **network, network, network.** Similar to getting your idea in front of people and getting your friends, colleagues, acquaintances and enemies on board with what you're doing, don't be afraid to recruit geniuses, experts and hard-workers from your immediate friendship circle or the circle beyond that. **The people you need to make your bullshit work are within touching distance of you right now. You just have to reach out to them.**

GET YOUR (BULL)SHIT TOGETHER

At this point I had the following things:
- A hangover
- A chef
- A sort of plan
- A waitress (my friend, Phoebe, an actress with waiting experience who, like Joe, completely understood what we were doing)
- A shed

I also had:
- A demand for my service
- The #1-rated restaurant in London
- A box of tea I didn't know what to do with???

And I knew I needed:
- Lights
- Seats
- Tables
- Atmosphere
- Ingredients
- Plates

But do you know what I didn't have?
- Any clue how I was going to make this work.

It's natural to have a wobble in the run-up to the launch of your big idea. In fact, it's arguable that I lived in a state of perpetual wobble in the six-week run-up to it. So far a lot of our focus has been on taking stock of where we are and what we're doing (where we are is **at the bottom**; where we want to get is **to the top**). Realizing that you're in a place you want to move up from can go one of two ways. It can be the motivator that makes you realise you really need to kick your ass into gear ('I don't want to wash my clothes with a washing machine full of shit anymore!'), or it can be the thing that completely ruins you and makes you feel like you're not worthy of the success you're aiming for ('Ah, who am I kidding? I'm just an idiot with a washing machine full of turds and sewage.'). But I'm here to tell you something I realized while preparing for The Shed, and the one motivator that has been at the core of my successes ever since:

Fear of failure is a powerful energy. Use it.

There's a central idea to everything I do, but I had to have my pre-Shed wobble to fully understand, identify and recognize it. From deciding to make The Shed a restaurant reality to the night of the actual launch, I had about six weeks. In that time, I almost quit a number of times. There were multiple voices of doubt, both in my head – I think 'doubting whether you can open a restaurant in the shed you live in without any prior restaurant experience' is, perversely, a sign of sanity; if I didn't question that I would be worried – and from the people around me.

Friends, co-workers, my girlfriend, my family; everyone in turn took their chance to quietly sit me down, look me in the eye with furrowed, knotted eyebrows, and go, "Hey, buddy: you, uh? You sure about this? You...you sure about this, bud?"

And in truth, the answer was: **no.**

I worried whether the food would work. Whether the bookings would dry up. Whether I could ever convincingly make my shed and the surrounding garden look like a rustic, pop-up restaurant experience. I worried that the first guest would turn up, take one look, say, "This is a joke, right?" then turn heel and go. I worried that all the work – by now, months worth of it – would have been for nothing. Did I worry whether this was stupid? A little, yes. But I mainly worried that, if I didn't do stupid **right**, I'd have nothing to show for it in the end.

At this point I want to introduce you to the most powerful idea in the book, and possibly in life:

The only way to make your idea work is to stop caring about your idea.

You have to treat your idea a little like a Tinder shag – exciting, intense, pure focus at the start, some middling-to-decent fore-play in the middle, then complete detachment and ghosting after you've bought it breakfast. I'll show you what I mean. Here's your two-step plan:

1. Have an idea that really, really, really excites you (and, crucially, passes the Bullshit Cortex)
2. Be pragmatic enough to treat that idea with complete disrespect

I know this is weird, but it's truly the genius at the center of all of this.

Your idea, when you first have it, is your precious baby son. You want to protect it at all costs, I understand that. You worry whether it has enough food, light, love and air. But you are also, in doing all this worrying, suffocating it. You cannot see a flaw in your own genius because you are too close to it to see its flaws. You're trying to paint the Mona Lisa with your nose to the canvas. And what you need is controlled distance – a cool air of detachment – that allows you to see your idea fully for what it is. **You need to be able to love it, then hate it. You need to be able to see it through other people's eyes.** Other people's criticisms are, often, valid. You just need to see them for yourself.

At a crucial point in the run-up to The Shed, I made an informed decision to detach myself from it and treat the idea with contempt. Recruiting Joe (and letting go of one of the key expectations of my idea as I did so) was a key part of that. Recruiting Joe taught me to be flexible, and bend around the hurdles in front of me rather than be defeated by them, and it let me zoom out from my idea and treat it pragmatically: if I failed, I would only fail because of the limits I had set **myself.**

And I think that is **the one, true, underlying reason for all the success that came with it:** being able to see it for the joke that it was and treat it as such. Suddenly, The Shed wasn't the Everything in my life. I was able to make cool, detached decisions without stressing over every minor detail. Approaching my idea like it was someone else's idea I was helping with allowed me to see the flaws, the upcoming difficulties, the things that wouldn't work and the things that would. I was able to get a 360 degree view on the whole thing from the safe, cozy vantage point of my own strange head.

TOOLKIT

So how do you stop, like, caring about an idea you've tried so hard to bring to fruition up until this exact moment? It's not easy, and this is the most difficult step of the entire process, but it's the one that offers the greatest reward, so take note. You have to trust the vision. I'll tell you how I do it, but keep in mind that for you, not all of these steps will necessarily make sense, so feel free to cherry pick from the list below and see which techniques work for you. Remember that there is no hard and fast way to stop caring (this section also works for people who've just had break-ups) (thinking of you xoxo).

STEP #1: LEARN TO INTERROGATE

Thankfully, we've already done this a little, back when we were fighting the negative backtalk coming from our **Bullshit Cortex.** A great way to learn to let go of an idea, or an ex, is to do some distracting side work on a project you've already put aside and abandoned – say, those chocolate-flavoured corn flakes we were thinking about earlier ('Choccies – The Corn Flakes That Are Brown!'™). Because you've already let go of the idea and convinced yourself that it's not worth pursuing any further, spending a day or even a long morning back on it again can give you a fresh perspective on the whole thing. It can actually be enjoyable to do work on an idea that doesn't have any weight attached to it, especially as a brief distraction from a project that you consider more significant. It feels more like playtime than work, and doing so can unblock whatever strangled feelings of creativity have inevitably come up when you're working on something important to you. Design the box, think how a TV advert might look, see if chocolateflavouredcornflakes.com is still available, think of spin-off flavours (hear me out: could cinnamon-flavoured chocolate-flavoured cornflakes work? Run it through the Bullshit Cortex!), then in the afternoon bring this refreshed attitude to your real idea. Can you sprinkle cinnamon on your restaurant-in-a-Shed? Not necessarily. But you're **thinking along the right lines.**

STEP #2: PUSH YOURSELF OUT OF YOUR COMFORT ZONE

We've already talked briefly about **recruiting the right people around you if you're not an expert in your field.** After returning to work on the corn flakes, I'd realized a few things. I'd need a chef to head up a test kitchen, someone with access to a corn-flake-pressing factory, a graphic designer to brand up the box, packaging and advertising art, and someone to run the sheer logistics of delivering hundreds of boxes of cursed mud-coloured cornflakes to reluctant supermarkets around the country. The **Push Yourself Out Of Your Comfort Zone** step means to take up one of those jobs and understand your idea from the perspective of a person who would be working on it. If you're a one-person operation, do the hardest, least exciting, slog part of your business. Spend a day generating invoices, for instance, and set little 30-day reminders in your calendar to chase up the ones that inevitably don't get paid. With The Shed, the sheer logistics of making it work bored me to tears, and it was in this mental space that I was able to look at the ceiling, laugh at the absurdity of it, and get out of bed, ready to face a new day with a renewed vigour for the whole idea. **Making something happen isn't always glamour and glitz.** Spend a day shovelling the bullshit and see what perspective it gives you.

STEP #3: GAMIFY YOUR BOREDOM

Gamification is something I believe in very deeply — and it's something we'll touch on in later chapters — as a way of motivating yourself and others to work harder, to extend the honeymoon period where you're in love with your idea, and to, crucially, offer a different **motive** for doing what you do — which, in turn, can give you a whole new perspective on **what you're doing and why you're doing it.**

With The Shed, the gamed motive behind it — getting to the #1 spot on TripAdvisor — was what fueled the early part of the plan. Having that simple goal in mind was all I had at the start. Once I'd achieved it, that was when I was able to see the idea as something bigger and turn it into the project that changed my life. There's a way to do this on a smaller scale, but it's something I've done in **every project I've worked on since.**

Step 3 is often reliant on Step 2. You're doing the most boring part of the process anyway, so make it a challenge to make it fun. How many invoices can you run in an hour, for instance? Why not take invoicing a step further and generate a spreadsheet to track each numbered invoice and give it a status — 'paid' or 'unpaid' — with a 'Date Due' section for when you can expect them to be fulfilled. Honestly, leave me to my own devices on a normal freelance day, and it can take me more than an hour to do one invoice. I just don't like that prickly asking-for-money section of the job, and I'll find up to a thousand small jobs to do first, even though the actual 'generate invoice, send polite email, schedule follow-up date' part of the task can only take a couple of minutes if I'm focused.

So shift the attitude. Turning it into a game – can I do five in, say, one hour? Can I reach out to ten new contacts on LinkedIn that could help with my job? Can I make five speculative phone calls? – gives you the motivation to work through the boring stuff. Once you've cleared your workload and seen, fundamentally, how easy it can be to have a clean deck, you have the renewed energy and headspace to laugh at your own idea. You see how easy it is when you just turn it into a game? The whole thing is absurd! Why are you worrying!

STEP #4: SHIT ON YOUR IDEA

This is where the Bullshit Cortex – plus a couple of other ominous voices of doubt – can come back in from the cold. I have something I run every project I do past called **'The Pub Test'**, and it's not particularly sophisticated: **if I'm nervous to explain the idea at the pub, or people look at me there as if I'm mad, then I'm on the right track.** If people aren't looking at me like I'm insane for even articulating the words coming out of my mouth, then **it isn't ambitious enough.** If they are? Well, then it's time to get the beers in.

At the early stage of something it can be hard to articulate what you're thinking. Young ideas are fragile and easily killed by scorn, and it's healthy and normal to want to keep them close and to yourself, like tiny baby model rabbits, until you're ready to release them into the wild. But talking them out in front of an audience uses the same tools required for **speaking them into existence.** The results, however, are the opposite side of the coin. Telling people what you're thinking and what you're doing opens you up to criticism and scorn, sure(the default human behaviour is to mock ideas, I don't know why this is), but **you can take that negative energy and those criticisms to help detach from your idea to make it a success.**

Here's an example. You want to launch a, uh...wooden whistle store. Your friend, Rob, tells you wood whistles are archaic and outdated. "The noise they generate is not in vogue in any form of modern music production!" he says. "Children won't want to learn the wood whistle!" Another friend, Geneva, agrees. "Wood whistles are primarily a hunting tool, like the ones that are designed to make duck sounds," she argues. "We're nowhere near any sort of bird-hunting ground right now. You'll be selling wood whistles to no one."

So OK, perhaps Rob and Geneva have shot down your idea, citing a lack of demand from two primary forms of wood whistle revenue. But what if you make wood whistles cool instead? What if your paint your wood whistles in bold, striped colours and set up an aspirational Instagram account where they look like modern decorative items? With the right combination of white marble, dusty pink and rose gold, you can sell wood whistles to interior design bloggers as the next du jour sideboard accoutrement. Send a few speculative whistles out to your favourite influencers! Make wood whistles the next must-have item! Get your wood whistles in your town's trendiest interior store! *Eliminate the need for your whistle to even make a sound at all.* And then take your wood whistle millions, and use them to **absolutely crush Rob and Geneva for ever doubting your vision.**

ADVENTURES IN BEING A BULLSHITTER

I think it's fair to say you bullshit a lot. You purchased this book. That's indicative of a trend in behavior. Sometimes you don't know you're doing it, but you are, constantly. Nobody is above bullshit. If you really want to get down to it, bullshitting is hardwired into the very nature of human psychology – taking that small nub of you that lives inside your head, that you know so well, and projecting it outwards, shooting it onto other people with a cloud of confidence, and thin air, and projection – that's bullshit. Every time you express the soul of yourself in any way outside of you through your mouth, you're technically bullshitting a little, just letting people know you're there by making some noise about it. **Don't be afraid of being a bullshitter.** It's happening all the time.

The first time I bullshat, it was a wild success. I was five years old. My family was taking a beach day, and our dad handed us all a shiny £1 coin to go and buy a toy to play with for the day. I, impulsively, bought a sort of ray gun thing, a tiny plastic pistol that made electric whirring sounds when you pulled the trigger. You know the ones. You had one as a kid as well. It was alright.

My cousin, however, went to the shop 20 minutes after us, and while she was there she managed to find a far greater prize: a plastic bow and arrow set (that could actually shoot!), and maybe I am hyping it up with my nostalgia but the bow was as big as she was and the arrow could fire for approximately one hundred million miles. I absolutely had to have it, but I had already spent my toy money. "Dad," I moaned, "Daaaad. Can I have another pound to buy a bow and arrow set?" And he said: **no.**

I want to make it clear that I have, with difficulty and a therapist's help, forgiven my father for his cheapness, but at the time

I was furious.

The oral history of this incident is hard to factcheck, but among my brothers it's pretty unanimously agreed upon that I went missing not long after this. I was from a large family (one of six siblings) so it was easy to slip away from the pack and go off and do your own thing. After a while, there was some mild parental concern about my whereabout – "Where's Oobah?" – that turned to a bigger group effort to find me – "Right, your brother's missing – everyone go spend five minutes trying to find him" – until, at the top of the beach, on the base of the promenade up to the shops and the parking garage standing above it, they found me, smirking and pale and topless, hands held neatly behind my back.

I was selling a seashell to a grown man for 20 pounds.

What had happened in the minutes since I'd disappeared was this: with a sandcastle bucket in hand, I had scoured the beach for treasures – a shiny pebble here, an interesting-looking shell there, a couple of tiny crabs dipped up out of a rockpool – and arranged them on my beach towel in the form of a shop front. Then, with great showmanship and a whole lot of formative bullshit, I started selling to passersby.

Would you buy an interesting shell from a 26-year-old man? You would: not. But back then, when I was just a cute, entrepreneurial little boy, the plan worked. Armed with my youth, my charm and my towel full of treasure, I managed to sell trinkets and sea gems and raised enough for one bow and arrow and an ice cream. The whole walk back to the car, my brothers covered in sea slime and sand, me eating and ice cream and firing an arrow into the sun, I beamed like the smug little goblin I was. **This was my first taste of bullshit, and I instantly craved more.**

When I was 15, me and a couple of my brothers were in a band. Obviously, nobody takes a band full of dish-faced teenage boys particularly seriously, so it was hard to secure any kind of paying gig anywhere in the surrounding area. We tended to play annual 'Battle of the Band' shows and the occasional pub-that-turns-a-blind-eye-to-underage-drinkers open mic night. That's until I came up with the bright idea of hiring Martin Davey.

Martin Davey was a gravel-voiced middle-aged cockney band manager, with a wealth of experience bringing local bands to the top and the gift of the gab to prove it. He also was just me, on the phone, pretending to be an old cockney band manager, calling up venues and fronting to them as if our band was good. And... it worked. Not every time, but most. Realizing that venues took bands more seriously when they had representation, I got us representation. It just also happened to be me, doing a voice, after watching one too many Guy Ritchie films.

This went well for a few months — we booked the kind of gigs that, sure, weren't going to have stadium rock bands shaking in their boots, but put us a couple of strides ahead of similar bands in our local scene. Then we made it to Madhouse, a big practice and rehearsal space in Birmingham, and that's where the scheme started to fall apart.

Turned out the venue was run in a kind of backwards way where all the bands appearing there had to pay a compulsory fee to play to cover the usual 'cost of putting a gig on' stuff, like security and staff and the hiring of the venue. I didn't understand that, because I was 15 and an idiot, and when my band and I turned up we were shell shocked that the venue's staff immediately asked where Martin Davey was. "He was supposed to pay us ahead of schedule!" they said. "You can't play without it!" I just shrugged indifference while they desperately called the mobile phone that was buzzing in my jorts pocket. "We just work with him," I said, innocently. "We don't know where he is."

In the end, we played, smashed it (according to the six to eight fans of ours who came to see our segment of the show, anyway), and after the show the desperate venue staff ended up apologizing to us for all the confusion. "And here's a band now," the announcer said, as we made it up onto the stage, "they've had a difficult night so far and I'm so sorry your manager's let you

down, boys...give them a big round of applause, it's The Meek!"
Once again, bullshit won out.

As my teen years progressed, I started to put a lid on these silly bullshit schemes of mine. That was due to a mix of things. There were voices of doubt around me, an internal nagging need to be seen as mature, the idea that abandoning such folly was a grown-up thing to do. **I plodded from my teens to early adulthood largely bullshit-free.**

And then I found myself in the rut I described earlier. You know, living in a shed, stagnant career, strange-smelling clothes. I was working for someone else doing work I didn't believe in and didn't feel anything for. I was making just about enough to get by but nowhere near enough to live comfortably. Bills were piling up, stresses and debts were piling up. I was, as I have detailed at length, *living in a shed.*

And then I met Georgio Peviani. And **my faith in bullshit was restored to me.**

MEET GEORGIO

I've always been fascinated by Britain's markets. It's important now to understand the difference between what the British call a market and a regular shop. Every city and town has one, and they are millions of miles away from the identical gloss of the rest of Britain's shopping complexes and high streets. Every shopping center in Britain is the same: two shops where you can buy sneakers, one enormous shop that moms very slowly walk around picking up cushions and then ultimately deciding not to buy cushions, two places to get a sandwich, and a cheap jewellers that nobody ever seems to go in.

Markets, on the other hand, are scrappy old wooden countertops and dangling barely-electric lights. In Brooklyn, they may be called bodegas. They are the scent of a deal and the knowledge that you can haggle. They are oddly branded European hammers in knife-proof plastic packaging next to a pile of ice with fresh mackerel laid out on it. Markets are fascinating, because they have a dark and interesting energy. There is always a man in a fannypack shouting about tomatoes.

And one stalwart of the modern British market is the knock-off clothing brand. Pierre Klein boxer shorts, Sergio Giorgini leather jackets, weird unlicensed t-shirts with Stewie Griffin saying a swear word on them. Not to mention the don of denim himself, Georgio Peviani.

I always wondered where the name 'Peviani' came from. I'd seen his denim at markets up and down Britain. His denim could be bought been back home, in Redditch, in the towns surrounding it, in Birmingham, the nearest city, and in London, once I moved here to find my fortune. Wherever I went, Peviani followed. I'd bought a couple of pairs of his jeans and they were more or less fine, for like £8. They wouldn't last too long and they weren't the most flattering cut, but they absolutely did the job they needed to - being pants. I always wondered about the formation of the name itself: was Georgio a real person? Had someone simply invented the name out of mid air? It seemed like it was meant to be as close to 'Giorgio Armani' as they could get without being sued. Had they gone through many other names before they landed on 'Peviani'? I smelled bullshit on Georgio Peviani, **and I liked what I smelled.**

I wondered if it was possible to take this name and make it something bigger. I was dying to know if it was possible to take the existing bullshit of Peviani and bullshit on top of it myself. I printed up business cards, registered a website, bought a pair of bright red 30" Peviani jeans and cut them off into abrupt little shorts. **And then I went to Paris Fashion Week in a pair of £8 jeans I bought off a market.**

Bluffing my way in was surprisingly easy. I simply bouffed my hair up into an eccentric coif, paired my bright red cut offs with more somber and fashion-y black denim jacket, wore shades for a minute or two too long when I was indoors, and introduced myself with unerring confidence. "Hi," I said, intensely shaking people's hands while slipping them my business card. "Georgio Peviani, designer."

I lingered near a couple of lines of people and quickly talked my way into the day's first runway show. There, as Peviani, I was emboldened enough to talk to the people around me. They invited me to follow them to the next show, an invite-only if-your-name's-not-down-you're-not-coming-in show that was only a cab ride away. "Will I get in?" I asked. "Please, Georgio," they told me. "You're with us. You'll walk right in." I stayed a step or two behind them as we all surged past the ominous looking bouncers, and that's how I ended up front row at a secret Vivienne Westwood show.

Fashion Week itself was heady. From Vivienne Westwood I went to more shows, as the day turned to the dark, and then, sweating at afterparties and afterparties to the after-afterparties. I spent some time on a bouncy castle with three-million Instagram follower model Alexa Chung. I was photographed with two mute fashion twins and the photo was picked up by the fashion press. I was stopped by fashion influencers who were broadcasting the whole event on Instagram live. "We're with designer Georgio Peviani," they said, to their hundreds of thousands of rapt followers. "Georgio, say hello." And with the half-English, half-continental eccentric voice I'd developed for the character of Peviani, I stared into the camera lens and whispered 'hi' across the world.

The Peviani glow lasted me all the way back to London. I was high on the fact that **I'd bullshitted myself into some of the most exclusive parties in the world, and nobody even questioned my jeans.** But I was no closer to figuring out who, if anyone, Georgio Peviani even was. I sat with my most meditative focus music playing ('lofi hip hop radio beats to relax/study to' on YouTube) and set about finding out. Like a hacker in the film Hackers, I tracked him down using complex and possibly illegal clandestine methods of information capture. By this I mean that I googled his name and found an old copyright claim on Page 3 of the results. It pointed me to an address in Aldgate, about a half-hour train ride from my house.

That's how I found myself in Denim World on Whitechapel Road, looking at the trove of Peviani styles around me. There were jeans and vests and jackets and overalls. There was every cut of denim you could imagine, distressed, coloured, tapered, flared. I asked at the customer service desk if Georgio Peviani worked there, and one by one they all demurred, pointing me around the shop to other people to talk to. Who was he? What was the mystery? Why all the subterfuge?

"Oh yes, that," Adam, the patriarch of the shop, said. I'd finally met someone with some answers in the jorts aisle. "Georgio Peviani doesn't work here, no. **I made him up 30 years ago.**"

Adam, see, was a born entrepreneur. He left Zambia in 1982 and travelled to Britain, and has been working in clothing ever since. At some point in the '90s, the name 'Georgio Peviani' came to him, and he's been operating under it ever since. "It sounded nice," he explained to me, "It sounded Italian." His favourite designer was Armani, and as he cribbed from him he found great success in the mid-'90s and early aughts. "That was 'Peak Peviani'," he told me. At its height, he was selling 35,000 Peviani pieces a week, worldwide.

"The thing I love about the brand is every Tom, Dick and Harry can afford it. It's not like Armani, where only certain elite people can afford them," he said. "It's been very successful for us. It's been what's kept this family and this business going all these years."

I told him all about my escapades in Paris and how I'd been passing myself off as Georgio Peviani. He keeled over with laughter, so I didn't feel the need to apologize too much, but then I realised something. Somewhere between me, Adam, and the fake name, Georgio Peviani existed. "You're Georgio Peviani, aren't you, Adam?" I asked him.

He burst into laughter, as did the colleagues who had by this point gathered around him.

"I'm as close as you'll ever find," he said.

TOOLKIT: FIND YOUR INNER GEORGIO

Well, how to turn this one into an instructable lesson you can apply to your life...uh, scour market stalls for a fake denim brand that sings to you? Con your way past security at an international fashion event? Wear red cut off shorts? No, none of this is good advice.

But what the whole Georgio Peviani escapade did was **made me fall in love with bullshit again.** It was silly, yes, and ridiculous, and beyond slightly heightened sales in knock off denim from Adam's Whitechapel store (some of my fans make a pilgrimage there to buy bootcuts and I have nothing but love for each and every one of them), there was no point to it. So what was the, well...point?

The point was that the birth of Georgio Peviani was the result of a rich lineage of bullshit that started on a beach in Aberdovey, made its way through a music venue in Birmingham and came full circle to me, smiling eerily at a very large bodyguard as he ushered me into a Westwood show at Paris Fashion Week. It also, it's important to mention, pre-dated The Shed. Because that idea, to make Peviani an it-boy in the fashion world, was the pilot light that ignited a much larger pile of flaming bullshit, and from there, everything went off. **Without Peviani, there is no Shed. With no Shed, there's no bullshit.** You wouldn't be reading this book now. Peviani's denim has a direct connection with the paper pages you are holding in your hand, right now. Unless you're reading this on some kind of e-reader, in which case...you know what, reword that analogy so it applies to whatever technology you're using to read this book.

Finding your Georgio isn't about finding a literal man called Georgio and taking him on as a mentor. It's about something deeper, something spiritual almost. Find the motivation, find the thing that gives you the energy to take your ideas through to fruition, do the dry run. Turn a small idea, like a snowball, into a big one, big enough to at least be the bottom third of a snowman's body.

Here's an example. Say you have a business, uh...**training pigs to sit like dogs.** It's niche work, admittedly, but the film industry might need it one day, and when that day comes you and 'Sit Down, Piggy' (the name of your business is 'Sit Down, Piggy', or 'SDP' on legal documents) will be ready to take advantage of the boom in demand. You never know when the world is going to need pigs to sit down like dogs on cue. No idea is a bad idea until that point.

So you've trained a couple of pigs to sit like dogs, cool. **Those pigs are your Georgios.** Take the energy you get from getting a pig to sit down, almost hauntingly, with its hind legs all bent and splayed, and turn it into the next idea: what else can you get pigs to do? Hop fences like a horse? Moo like a cow? Or, maybe, find out what other animals can you train to sit that way. Maybe there is something to be said for a goat that can kick field goals. A donkey that can smile. Before you know it, you've got a field full of ugly, monstrous creatures doing a whole bunch of things that spit in the face of God. And most importantly, you've got a much bigger idea than what you started with.

If you do launch SDP, I want 10% shares when the pig-sitting boom finally comes to us, and my own horse that can rap. This is my idea until it is yours.

POWERFUL STUFF

It's time to realise the power of your idea. Because so far we've done the following:

- Had an idea
- Run it past the Bullshit Cortex (and, if not leapt the hurdle, at least worked through it quickly enough to maintain some momentum)
- Started work on what we're doing
- Recruited friends, family and enemies around us to the cause
- Detached and interrogated the idea enough to realise all the flaws it has

But what we haven't done is given ourselves an electric shot-in-the-arm of belief. A lot of what we've done so far has focused on **speaking things into existence** – the central thesis of this book and most of my work is **'bullshit enough and it will turn into something'.** Speaking is a good start, but belief, that iron-solid foundation at the base of every idea you have, the internal balancer on which you can build everything, needs to be there.

Essentially, it comes down to this: Where do I get the confidence to bullshit from? And how do I give that confidence to you?

Firstly, we need to understand why we need to believe in ourselves. A lot of my ideas start as little pots that I put on the small burner – The Shed, for instance, initially began as a review rigging exercise, and it didn't rule my life until the very end. For the most part, it was short, sharp increases of activity that kept the pot boiling. It wasn't something that took over my every working day. It was something I worked my life around. I did a lot of other, unrelated things while I was working on The Shed until the idea became so big that I couldn't ignore it anymore.

Why didn't I quit? Why didn't I stop doing that when I didn't immediately get anywhere? Why didn't I listen to the voices of doubt from my Bullshit Cortex and almost everyone I spoke to, and allow them to discourage me? **Because I believed my own bullshit.**

The same goes for Peviani. When I found myself confronted with a burly bouncer outside a fashion show to which I patently wasn't invited, my pale and ugly knees knocking in the frigid Parisian wind, why didn't I just shy away, apologize, turn around and go home? **Because I believed enough in my idea to make it happen.**

Voices of doubt come from all sides, but **the loudest one is always inside your own head.** As we've seen previously, that voice of doubt can be recast into a powerful tool. But when we're trying to build a rock-solid foundation of belief in oneself, it can be your worst enemy. Think of your mind like a meadow full of garbage. Clear the litter (the voice of doubt) and allow the green shoots of grass (your idea) to push through. You don't need to throw all of the garbage away. There might be gold in that garbage, or a hard drive full of Bitcoin, which for some reason people are always throwing away. But you do need to move it for a bit to make your confidence grow.

TOOLKIT

Listen, I can't give you a simple shortcut to self-confidence. Sometimes you either have it or you don't. But those people who naturally swagger around full of self-confidence? So often, it gets mistaken for arrogance. Being confident in your ideas is great but it can quickly turn dangerous if you unthinkingly believe in everything you do. When doubts come up, there are four techniques I like to use to work through them, but the most important one is this piece of knowledge: real **self-confidence is built on doubt.** If you can acknowledge flaws, holes, problems or fears, stare them in the eye and work through them, then you **know** your idea is good and solid and worth pursuing. If your idea can survive a few doubts, it is bulletproof.

1. VISUALIZE A FUTURE WHERE YOU DIDN'T LISTEN TO YOUR DOUBTS

I know this sounds so straightforward, but close your eyes and imagine the exemplar, successful version of you in five years. Imagine you, standing at the top of a skyscraper, staring out at the city below you. Imagine you, throwing simply hundreds of thousands of dollars at a stripper, so much that the stripper is like, "Sir are you sure you want to be spending this much money right now?" The stripper had to get a special broom to sweep all the money up with. "Sir it was a four-minute dance. I know I'm good at my job but this seems excessive. I just don't want you to have buyer's remorse." Imagine you, stood in a field red with blood, the severed heads of your vanquished enemies below you. Or, you know, think smaller. Imagine you, sat in front of your bustling eBay online store, inventorying your stock and merrily fulfilling a steady trickle of orders. Then think of yourself in the same situation a few years forward. History doesn't have pretty pictures of the doubters. If you listen to and live the version of your life that your doubt wants you to lead, it's just you, sitting in front of a window on a grey day, sighing at what could have been. It's straightforward, it's simplistic, but it works: **visualisation is a powerful tool for motivation.**

2. CONTEXTUALIZE YOUR DOUBT

If you listen to your doubt, who is it going to affect most? The answer is you. Doubt isn't a thoughtful friend trying to do the best by you and help you avoid embarrassment. It's a wicked whisper designed to keep you away from your own success. Zoom out a bit. Will your doubt matter the same way in six months, a year, five years, twenty? Will your doubt die with you, or will it stop you from leaving a legacy? In a hundred years, will people talk about that person who sat on the sofa and doubted themselves into inactivity? Or will they talk about that strange blonde man who made a restaurant out of his shed? That's a trick question. The only thing people on earth will be talking about in a hundred years is, like, 'which of the six remaining survivors will we kill and eat next' or 'do you think aliens will come and save us from the waves'. Nobody will be talking about either of us, because they'll be on fire. But it's good to think about, all the same.

3. RECOGNIZE THAT DOUBT CAN BE IMPORTANT

Doubt is there to trick you. Simply ignoring it won't make it go away. The way to deal with doubt is head-on. Acknowledge your doubts, but don't invest any time and energy into them. Write them all down on sugar paper and eat them all up. Scream your doubts into a fire. Write them in the dirt on a van, then erase them with the spray of a hose. Doubts are tests. Look them in the eye, say "Thank you, doubt, you have served your purpose," then dismiss them. That's a powerful move.

4. TAKE HEART FROM THE FAILURES OF OTHERS

...and yourself. Remember at the start of this book, where I was? Shed, washing machine, foxes shagging beneath my house, dead-end job, girlfriend very rapidly getting mad at me re: my life's complete lack of momentum? We've all been there. A big part of this book is inventorying your own rock bottom, identifying the low you never want to return to. Everyone who has ever been a success was a failure way before that. Building self-confidence comes from knowing that. Failures are good and natural. They happen to the best of us. But the only way to be defeated and let failure win is to allow yourself to be conquered by the pain it inflicts. You've been thrown from a horse. Are you going to stand up, dust yourself off, and inelegantly kick one leg over its saddle again? Or are you going to lie in the dust and dirt and allow it to trample you to death? **That horse is doubt.**

VOICES OF DOUBT
(OR: STOP LISTENING TO OTHER PEOPLE'S BULLSHIT)

I want to make one thing very clear, because there have been a lot of lies flying around. **Yes, a number of people in my life told me that opening a restaurant in my Shed was a bad if not terrible idea.**

My girlfriend, when I told her the idea: "No. Absolutely not."

My most cherished group chat, en masse: "What? You're doing what?"

My brother, Pete: [quietly] "I'm not sure that's... such a good idea, Oobah."

My landlord: "[I did not tell my landlord in case he vetoed the whole thing and evicted me]".

My girlfriend, again, still going: "But where am I going to sleep? You cannot expect me to sleep in a restaurant." She was right, and I got her a hotel. They were all right, in a way.

We've faced the voice of doubt in our own heads, but this chapter is about the voices of dissent around you, because there are going to be some. I now take a small point of pride in making people blink slowly twice, recoil back for a moment, take a sip of their drink as they think how best to tell me I'm being an idiot, and then quietly say, "Oobah...". It means I'm doing something right. It's not always a hard rule, but it's one I live by nonetheless: **if you're not pissing people off, you're not being ambitious enough.**

But it's taken me awhile to get there. Sometimes it can be hard to ignore an onslaught of negativity. If people aren't as invested in your idea as you are, they are naturally going to be questioning of it. It's human nature, especially among my fellow Brits, to see an idea and, instead of embracing it, instantly undermine it. People questioned Martin Davey the cockney band manager, and Georgio Peviani. They questioned me when I was simply asking them to fill out reviews on TripAdvisor. **I didn't expect people to back my biggest idea without questioning it.**

When the voice of doubt is in your head, it's easier to face it because it's local and familiar. You can have an argument with yourself and, that way, you always win. When the voice of doubt takes the form of another person, it can be trickier.

In the lead up to the launch of the restaurant, I'll admit that those voices started to get to me, and added power to the looping doubt-track that was already playing in my head: **is this too silly to work? Am I going to embarrass myself? Are people immediately going to find me out, and question me to my face? Can I pull it off? Should I cancel it now?**

It was undermining my confidence, until I realized that I always did this. When I did Peviani, was there a chorus of doubters? Yes. When I was playing Martin Davey on the phone, did people think I was being stupid? Yes. But when I pulled the stunts off, were those very same doubters the first people to pat me on the back and congratulate me? **Absolutely.**

People don't mean to be malicious when they doubt you. In many ways, people express their doubts about my ideas because they don't want to see me get hurt by the failure that they see as inevitable. And I completely recognize and appreciate that they want to protect me from making a fool of myself.

But if you think it doesn't taste doubly sweet to prove every single one of those doubters wrong with every atom of my success, you're wrong.

This makes me sound very 'I marched across mountains to conquer the Romans,' I understand that. It makes me sound like 'my brother very mildly doubting me in the pub' was akin to an ancient war. But it feels great to win. And it feels doubly great to prove people wrong.

If people are doubting your bullshit, that's a sign you're onto something. That means you have two things that are important. You have the motivation to prove them wrong and a multiplier on every drop of success you get as a result of not listening to them. **Learn to love doubt.**

THE MOMENT OF SUCCESS

I want to tell you the story of how I actually made The Shed happen, the day that I actually turned my house into a restaurant. But first we need to take a few steps backwards, through the frantic days before.

I was working with the media company VICE to make a video of the experience (it is highly likely that you have seen this video; as of the exact moment of me typing this, 41.4 million people have), which meant that a lot of people were involved in the production of it, which meant that we had a fixed and immovable date. We were locked in to a Friday night in the middle of a freezing November. There could be no rescheduling it, no swerving it out of the way.

Having cameras and people filming the night was easy to explain away. My restaurant had been top of the TripAdvisor chart for some weeks now – we simply told diners they were recording a documentary about the #1-rated restaurant in London and, for the inconvenience, their meal that night would be free. This was good for two reasons. It meant that I didn't feel bad about charging people for frozen food I'd simply reheated from a supermarket, and it meant that I didn't have to ever buy a card machine to process credit card payments, because those are very expensive.

Having a fixed date meant I knew the exact day my idea would live or die, which absolutely ramped up the anxiety over whether it would work. Again, if I hadn't already worried that I might not be able to convince people my shed was a restaurant, I think that's a worry worth having. Even your best idea can be subject to doubts. As the date got nearer, I definitely had mine.

I had one goal in mind. I was going to convince every person who had made a booking at The Shed that the restaurant was real. If even one person looked around, noticed the complete lack of infrastructure, and quietly asked me if it was a joke — or, my worst fear, that someone would stand up and shout "THIS ISN'T REAL!" — all those months of work and pressure would be for nothing.

To do that, I needed to prepare the restaurant. As per the reviews, diners were expecting to sit outdoors. I'd phoned up three of the more frequent callers to the restaurant and asked if they could make the booking. One man, the most surprised of all, actually said "I can't believe it's real!". Sir, you were more correct than you'll ever know. I basically made a restaurant just for you. So I tidied the garden and borrowed some furniture. A pub up the road, where a friend of mine tended bar, agreed to lend me some heaters to place in the outdoor space.

Then I needed to make The Shed **seem real**, and there's definitely a Bullshit Lesson in there somewhere. Marketing can be anything and everything for a small business or idea. Just like when I was playing at being Georgio Peviani, when I had printed up business cards and handed them out with a placid smile, in this instance I recruited friends to sit at tables around the 'restaurant' having their own meals and conversations. That way, when the real guests arrived, they wouldn't be confronted with an empty restaurant that would arouse their suspicions. They'd assume other people were having a good time, and they'd be more likely to have a good time. Is this idea a bit like back-alley three card monte dealers, paying crowds to gather around their stall to hook in innocent paying members of the public? Yes, sort of. Did it work regardless? Also yes. **Do not be afraid of the dark arts of bullshit.**

Third, we needed atmosphere. As per the reviews my friends had already written, people were expecting an al fresco, performance-based service — thankfully, this is not unusual in London. A friend of mine, DJ Sambience, set up a booth at the back of the garden area to play actual recorded ambient restaurant noise, with a 'ding!' timer set up to occasionally cover the noise of the actual microwave pinging in the kitchen behind him. And my actress friend Phoebe was on hand to greet diners, give them the intense service industry experience, and tell them what food they should order based on mood. We didn't even have to get menus printed up.

Then there was the food itself. Remember I told you how I recruited the chef in the first place, at 6 a.m., slick with sweat and jetlagged, talking to a friend-of-a-friend? This was not a professional operation. Since early that morning, Joe had been with me in the kitchen making up the menu, after we'd gone into town a few hours earlier and bought our supplies. With his background as a professional chef, he was able to plate up an Iceland frozen vegetable lasagna to look Michelin-starred. He placed edible flowers on the top of the scab-like cheese crust. He'd made a Cup-a-Soup in teacups to make it look more haute cuisine. He'd even prepared a dessert, which was three Ferrero Rocher in a mug with whipped cream. With the chaos swirling around them, nobody knew that this food was, well, trash. It looked like a restaurant, smelled like a restaurant, sounded like a restaurant. Why wouldn't they believe it was a restaurant?

VERY BRIEF TOOLKIT

Listen, say you've set up a, uh...stall selling artisanal jelly. Raspberry, that sort of thing. Persimmon. You don't just turn up with a few screw-top jars you've soaked the labels off and try and sell them like that, do you? You hire a market stall, you print up a canvas stall banner ('John's Jellies!' the banner says [in this example, your name is John]. 'Best Jellies in Town!'). The jelly labels themselves are printed and applied neatly and with care. You don't pile your stall with every jar of jelly you have. You make neat little stacks, three at the bottom, then two, then one on top, in a pyramid, with little handwritten signs describing the jelly flavour notes and the price. You dress it, essentially, like a fancy soap store. And do you do that because you're lying? No. Do you do that because you're a jelly expert, and you know everything there is to know about jelly? No, that is impossible; jelly is a preserve with infinite possibilities. But you do it like that because **you're bullshitting people into thinking what you're doing is more real than it is.** And that's not bullshit, not really. That's selling an idea. Because if you sell your idea once, you have more money to sell your idea again. And that's how ideas really get going. Jelly stalls and ambient restaurant music. They're all the same half-lie.

BACK AWAY FROM JELLY AND ONTO THE SHED AGAIN

The final piece of the puzzle was Trevor, the chicken man. Again, I had artistic license to play with here, thanks to all my friend's reviews. I thought filling the spare storage house in the garden of my shed with some tame chickens, tended to by their handler, Trevor, would give the restaurant a suitably bizarre feel. Guests were invited to choose a chicken they might like to eat, like you would a lobster from a tank in a fancy restaurant, a gambit I knew would work without us needing to kill a chicken because who on this planet would do that? Trevor turned up late, in a massive sheepskin coat and with an erratic chicken-charged energy, and I knew he was the perfect element of disruption in my poised plan. A man in the corner of a garden, tending to a fire pit and quietly cooing at chickens, was, bizarrely, the exact thing I needed to convince my guests that this restaurant was real.

And then the guests arrived, and I shit myself.

Up until then, I'd been confident. As the night fell and the garden transformed into a hushed, lamplit nirvana with patron-less tables of lasagna dotted around it, even I had convinced myself this was a convincing mimicry of a viable restaurant. But when I got the first call from guests around the corner (I didn't give away the restaurant's exact address so that no one could look it up and see I was lying about it existing), my stomach dropped to my feet. This was it. No turning back.

Leading guests blindfolded through my garden towards the

shed was the most nerve-jangling experience of my life. And then I asked them to remove the scarves tied round their eyes, and... they looked around and said "Wow!" I walked them to their tables. Around them, stooges dressed as high-faluting restaurant customers ate soup from a mug. The real guests shuffled their chairs closer to where they'd be eating, jostling the legs over clods of grass. Phoebe went and offered them wine. They...didn't seem to think anything was wrong? They...didn't shout at me, angry for having been fooled? They...accepted the restaurant as truth?

The first couple who turned up were local. They asked me how often the restaurant opened, how they kept walking around nearby trying to figure out where it was, questioned me on the finer details of the neighborhood, thanked me for taking their booking. The second couple who arrived were from out of town, a sweet American couple, on vacation in Europe, who had dined the night before at a Michelin-starred restaurant in the twinkling heart of Paris. After a day spent on the Eurostar to London – and down deep into the heart of south-east London, where I lived, which is just as much of a journey – they took their blindfolds off with trepidation. Were they about to out me?

"We don't have anything like this in the US," they said, as I bought them mugs of hot soup. "This is so interesting. What an experience." They...liked it? They...assumed all restaurants were like this in London? They...seemed to be having a nice time?

By this point I was euphoric. But the third and final set of guests were possibly the hardest to please of all. They were a party of three who had emailed their reservation from a famous London fashion house, possibly scouting the restaurant ahead of reserving it for their glamorous, tastemaking boss. If anyone was going to turn around and tell me my garden full of space heaters was a joke, it was going to be them. Cautiously, I led the three of them, hands chained together, through the garden. They removed their blindfolds. Trevor let a chicken flap near one of the women, who it turned out had a pathological fear of the animals. And then they...sat down and ordered wine?

The night moved in a blur. Joe kept the food pinging out of the shed kitchen. DJ Sambience kept the ambient mood music playing. Phoebe perfectly kept each table attended and, crucially, a little bit tipsy. My stooge friends played their parts perfectly. They were all scheduled to leave at different intervals so the tables could be turned, like a real restaurant. By the end of the night, I was forgetting I was even doing this as a joke. I flitted from guest to guest. "Are you having a nice time?" I asked them. "It's very cool," one couple said. "Does this mean it'll be easier for us to book again?"

At the end of the night, two of the three tables asked to make another reservation (the American couple declined to as they were flying back the next day). I'd pulled it off. **I made seven restaurant-loving strangers believe my Shed and back garden were the top-rated eatery in London.** And none of them suspected a thing.

WHY SUCCESS IS TERRIFYING

If I thought the euphoria of pulling off the night was a high, I had no idea what I was in for. Success came in two waves. After writing an article for VICE explaining what I'd done, I was in for a whirlwind day of press coverage. I appeared on Britain's biggest morning TV show, Good Morning Britain, where presenter Susanna Reid called me a "very naughty boy." I was featured on new shows in Australia and the US, and every newspaper in England, and many in the US, wrote about what I'd done and requested interviews with me. People saw my trick as a sort of elaborate "Fuck you" to TripAdvisor and online ranking systems as a whole. That I'd managed to scam my way to the top of one, and get people down to my pitiful shed to eat, was seen as a huge pie in the face to all these lists that we rely on every time we Google where's good to get a coffee, or the best sandwiches in our city. I appreciated the sentiment, but most of all I was buzzing that I'd pulled it off. If the shell-selling of my youth, the Martin Davey character, and the Georgio Peviani wheeze are anything to go by, I'm never motivated solely by proving a point. **I'm motivated by being a bullshitter, and I'd just proved myself as the biggest one in the country.**

Then, a month or so later, the video came out, and the reaction was a hundred times what it was before. Millions of views stacked up overnight. I was interviewed by Japanese TV, and debated as a prankster in Singaporean parliament, which, given how corrupt their government is, is quite the achievement. I was so busy and overwhelmed with emails that I missed the Washington Post's request for an interview. ITV just came to my house because they had no better way of getting in touch with me. I did a full 24 hours of TV in countries on four continents. The Shed's trap phone, which I'd neglected to disconnect, was ringing all day. People from around the world phoned me up to just say "legend" into the phone. I've been to Bangladesh, Sweden, San Francisco, a yacht liner for CEOs and billionaires, hosting conferences and telling my story. I've missed taxis that have been waiting outside my house to take me to an airport because another taxi has already been taking me to a different airport. **I, perhaps most importantly, no longer live in a shed.** The idea was the biggest of my life. I've turned it into extraordinary success.

That success, though, doesn't mean it's not scary. In the first flurry of activity after the Shed story broke, I was totally overwhelmed by it. I was on the train to see a friend and went into a long tunnel. By the time I got out of it, I'd had 40 missed calls from members of the media. At 5 a.m. the taxi came to my house to take me to the Good Morning Britain set, and I had an anxiety attack trying to find clothes. I had no clean clothes! I hadn't expected this! People were coming up to me in public to tell me what a legend I was – thank you, correct – and I was too busy trying to find an exit so I could find a quiet place to breathe to graciously accept their praise. When the taxi was idling outside and I was picking jumpers off the floor and smelling them, I had a realization.

I couldn't back out now.

This is what I'd wanted, right? I'd wanted my idea to be a success; I'd wanted my bullshit to pay off. I wanted the adulation, the fame, the people calling me a genius. But suddenly my brain was in fight or flight mode. What if I just cancelled the interview? It was too late to back out. This had become bigger than I was. Suddenly, I was The Shed guy. The biggest idea of my life had become my life. And that's good, now – I mean, I'm writing a book telling you how great success is – but back then, in the morning cold of my shed with a jumper on and no clean trousers, it was terrifying. Overnight, my life had been redefined by a new level of success. **I'd bullshitted my way to the top but I hadn't prepared myself for it.**

Sometimes it still happens now. I still get the voice in my head, the leftover voice of doubt, whispering, "What are you going to do, not do it?" There are TV appearances I am nervous for. Meetings with successful people in the industry. I was invited to one of my heroes houses for dinner, and nearly dropped out at the last second. I thought, 'he doesn't want to meet me, really! Who are you fooling! Go home!' But in the end the night was fantastic. We got wine-drunk at his beautiful home and ate outside by a fire pit, truly Shed chic. Doubting yourself is human, as we've already learned. But it doesn't go away once you succeed. **You just learn new ways to bullshit yourself.**

To return to an old tool: so what? So what if this doesn't work? It's better to go down trying than fail without even finding out what you're capable of.

MAKING SUCCESS THE NEW NORMAL

I realized something recently, while I was stood on a stage in Bangladesh wearing a custom-fitted suit and making a presentation to hundreds of people in front of printed banners with my big pale face stretched to the size of a family car: **I'd made it.**

I was thousands of miles, literally and figuratively, from two years before, when I'd been awake in the blue-black dark of the night, listening to foxes shag and wondering where near my house I could buy non-sewage stained clothes.

After the conference, a small line of attendees waited to speak to me. Offer praise, ask a few words of advice, pose for photos, shake my hand. A couple of businessmen invited me out to dinner afterwards and I, alone in a strange country, gladly accepted. They took me to a beautiful restaurant, an actual one, with indoor seating, and treated me to one of the finest meals of my life. We were up until the early hours, cornered in a mostly empty five-star restaurant while the staff tidied around us, drinking fine wine, laughing and smoking cigars. I went to sleep in the beautiful hotel the conference had bought for me, and woke up smiling between crisp white linen sheets.

This happens a lot these days. I've been the last man standing at restaurants in Oslo and Paris. I've been shown the sights of New York. I've opened the curtains on the 25th floor of hotels and stared down at the twinkling city below me. I've made friends from strangers who already know my name. I've tasted wines that cost more than my rent, even my rent post-Shed. I've eaten meals that chefs have made especially for me, peeking out of their kitchen to nod at me and shake my hand. I've posed for photos I've never even seen. I've had groups of people stop me in the street to tug at the thigh of their Peviani jeans and tell them they wear them because of me. It feels great. I cherish every moment. I realize and fully appreciate how rare and how special it is.

But up on that stage, telling my story, I paused twenty minutes in. The Shed has taken over the last year of my life. It's taken me around the world, fed and clothed me. It's made my the success I am today.

But that's not the end of it.

Success is wonderful, and it's easy to wallow in it. I mean this, again, literally. There is nothing quite so luxurious as a hotel bath filled with two little things of Aesop shower gel. There's just something special about a bath when you're not paying the water or heating bill. But it's also easy to forget why you craved success in the first place. It's easy to get a little too comfortable, and let your guard down. It's easy to think you've made it when you've climbed a few rungs up from where you started, forgetting that there's still a long ladder left to climb if you want to climb it. Am I happy being a success? Absolutely. I'm the happiest I've ever been in my life. Do I want to climb further, go higher, make even more businessmen in strange companies buy me dinner? Yes I do. I want this level of success to be my new baseline. I want this success to be my new low that every high is hereby measured against. And that means inverting one of the most powerful tools that got me here.

MAKING THE BULLSHIT CORTEX WORK FOR YOU

Up until now, we've had to dismiss the voice of doubt – both the one that lives in your head, also known as the Bullshit Cortex, and the one that spills out of your friends, family, employers, enemy, and that boy in the coffee shop down your road who never entirely seems comfortable when you're talking to him and telling him all your plans but you do it anyway because he has a kind face and an easy manner and he's too afraid to ask you to stop, even if he has started questioning you, as your latte grows cool in your hand.

As we've covered, criticism and doubt can be good, but it can also undermine your self-belief, holding you back from getting to the place you're going.

Save this chapter until you've followed the advice in the rest of the book, had an idea, interrogated it, made it perfect, made it real, then made it a success. **Bookmark this page and come back to it.**

OK, done that? Great. You're ready now.

We need to listen to the Bullshit Cortex again so you don't get too carried away with your massive success.

Listen, you and I are alike now. We enjoy the finer things, people fawn over us and tell us we're amazing, and, very truly, we are. We know how good life can be because we've made that for ourselves.

But now that we're a success, people have stopped questioning us. They don't see flaws in our ideas, because **we** had them. **Every single 'no' you ever got coming up has turned to a 'yes' in the context of your success.** Now, people don't tell you that you're wrong, or you could fail. They tell you you're going to be brilliant because you've already proved to them that you are.

This is a dangerous place to be in. It's not people's fault: those around you don't set out to be **Yes Men**, just as they never tried to be **No Men** in the first place. But the echo chamber telling you how amazing you are is just as poisonous to your ideas as the one that told you that you were wrong before. **The Voices of Doubt have turned into The Voices of Absolute Confidence.**

Both are equally dangerous and important to address. Please, someone hand this section of the book to Kanye West.

TOOLKIT

Let's say you started a business that...well, it's an app that's like Tinder, but it pairs people up based on what part of the pizza they like to eat best. Some like the inner pizza, with the cheese and the toppings. Some like the crusts, to dip in garlic sauce. You swipe left to find someone who has the same interests as you, but prefers the part of the pizza you usually leave. Then you meet up to watch a film and share a pie. I want to be very clear about this: users are not encouraged to start romantic relationships based on this. This is not a hookup app. It's just so people can make friends in new cities and go halves on an 18" together without the waste. The app is called 'Pizzer'.

So say you started that. Do you know how to code an app? No. You found a coder. You started a word of mouth campaign among family and friends to be the first users. You spoke to local pizza restaurants to offer discount codes to your user base, and from there they cut you in on the sales. As the face of Pizzer, you've become famous and rich beyond your wildest dreams. They gave you a marinara sauce endorsement. There was an advert starring you that ran for a full minute during the Super Bowl.

But along the way people have started believing in every move you make. In the bath in your fancy hotel room, you have an idea: Burriter. What if people could meet up and buy burritos together? They wouldn't be able to share them in the same way because...I mean you can't share a burrito, can you, it's a mess. It's not like some people prefer to eat the tortilla (commonly known as the 'burrito skin') while others prefer to eat only the fillings. But people can still make friends. It's a social food! Mexican restaurants could cut you in with the voucher code. You could make another billion off this idea!

Who's going to tell you no? Nobody. They've seen you make ideas into success stories before. They're going to trust you to do it again. **This is a terrible idea, but nobody dares to tell you.** Or worse, they have blind faith that you've actually had a good idea, and you're going to bring them down when you fail.

This is when you need to take the Bullshit Cortex off that long beach holiday it's been on and start to doubt yourself again. Get that same old notebook out you used to defeat it before, and start another list of pros and cons. PRO: Burritos are a social food. CON: They are not really shareable. CON: Adult friendship apps are niche anyway. Adults are very icky about making friends. CON: Would you make friends with someone who had sour cream around their mouth, carnitas juice on their hands and fingers, and who very urgently needed to undo the top button of their pants because they ate too much burrito too quickly and now they are full and gassy? No. There are too many CONs to this one. Cancel this idea. This is a real chocolate cornflake of an idea.

Maybe you still have some friends who are straight with you, regardless of your many glimmering achievements. Treasure them. The Voice of Doubt on your way up can be your greatest ally when you're at the top. Enjoy your success, but with a caveat: **never forget that you're still fallible.** Keep the voice of doubt near you, and the Bullshit Cortex bubbling, for the next time you really need them. They might just save your ass.

CHEER UP, THOUGH

Here's a fundamental thing I've learned on my journey, and one I can tell you now but you'll figure out first for yourself: **it feels good to change your life with ordered and positive thinking.**

Heck, I didn't especially set out to succeed in the way I did. A lot of my success came from following instincts, knowing when to not listen to a "no", a heap of luck and a huge amount of hard work – but it still feels good to succeed by trusting yourself, listening to yourself, and thinking in a new and different way.

Whenever I get too ahead of myself, I like to think that I could just not be here. **I could have done nothing, and still be living in a shed with the foxes and the washing machine** (I'll get over the washing machine soon, I promise)(in actuality it only happened two, maybe three times)(critics will say I should have emailed my landlord if I had a problem and not write and produce an entire self-help book based on it)(those critics are Bullshit Cortexes made flesh, and should be dismissed).

But I didn't. I had an idea. I got people to help. I scraped up enough momentum to make something happen. I followed my instincts. I learned to let go of my expectations in a way that was integral to the success of my strategy, and still very positive to me. I learned to treat my idea with the contempt it needed to be a success. **I made a winner out of myself.**

And on whatever scale you do that, it feels good.

I still rent The Shed. I use it as the office for my production company. It helps to remind me the base level I used to live at, and thought I was happy at (and, in complacency, was).

But it also reminds me of how far I've come. It serves as a reminder to me that I don't want to go back there. It's a monument to the fact that I changed my way of thinking, and turned my life around.

I wasn't a success, and then I was. And that was all down to one idea.

One plan.

One bit of luck going my way.

One feeling of elation that I wanted to chase.

One motive.

One ending.

Your 'one' can be anything. It's a small victory along the way. It's a single person believing in your idea when you're starting to waver. It's the first jar of jelly you sell, or box of chocolate-flavoured corn flakes. It's the first download of an app that isn't from your friend who you've specifically told to download your app.

There is power in 'one.'

I still celebrate little victories along the way. **I still delight when people tell me my ideas are silly or pointless.** Those moments are like successes to me because I know I can prove them wrong. It's one more atom of motivation. One more doubt I can use as fuel, pushing me to work harder. One more success waiting to happen.

But sometimes I also sit back and ask myself an important question, a question that's important in all of life, but one that comes with success more than it does with failure:

Am I a dickhead though?

THE DICKHEAD TEST

I meet more successful people now than I did when I lived in a shed in south London. This is just simple mathematics. I go to conferences and attend events designed for successful people to learn even more success from people who have succeeded in new or unusual ways.

Because of the platforms I am given, I am exposed to more successful people than I was before.

Many of them are very nice. I can learn from them as much as they can from me, they are generous with their time and their wealth, and also a lot of successful people for some reason really smell good. I think it's something to do with being so rich they can buy cologne or perfume from a shop, rather than duty free, and they are much more careless and easy about spraying it on themselves? Maybe it's that?

(Honestly, if you take anything away from this book, it should be to spray one or two more puffs of a nice scent on yourself each morning before you leave the house. If you **smell** like a successful person, **success will follow.**)

But some successful people aren't so hot. They're arrogant, and rude. They think those that aren't on their level are beneath them. They're selfish, and think their voice should be the loudest in the room. **Sure, their necks and pulse points smell nice. But their attitudes stink.**

The first time I met a Successful Dickhead, I was disappointed. "Aren't you happy to be on top?" I thought to myself. "Do you not get a kick from being up where you weren't before? Don't you want to share that wisdom, knowledge, and good feeling?"

But some people don't want to be like that. They revel in their

own success. They think there's only room for them at the top table, and anyone else trying to succeed is a threat to them. Sometimes they can't even be nice to the people who pose no threat
to them, people who aren't working towards similar goals, like a
waitress in a restaurant who can't control how fast the food is
prepared and is simply trying to do her job.

Sure, they're a success. But they're a brat. They're an asshole.
People say mean things behind their back.

And I never want to be one of those.

Sometimes you have to stop and ask yourself the difficult
questions. Am I a good person? Am I of net positive worth to the
spinning of the planet? When I leave this life, will the people around
me be better off for me having been here, or worse?

And most importantly:

Am I a dickhead?

TOOLKIT

I can't tell you whether you're a dickhead. Well, I theoretically
could. But I'd have to meet you. I'd have to start charging for that
service. I will come to your house, sit with you for 45 minutes or an
hour, share with you a cup of coffee or a sandwich, and, at the end,
review whether you're a dickhead as per my own preferences and
criteria. This service will cost you $15,000. You can ask the peo-
ple around you if you're a dickhead, but people tend to say "err...?"
for a really long time until their voice starts creaking when you ask
them directly, "Listen: am I a dickhead or not?" And usually, the
people who are dickheads are too self-assured to even wonder if
they might be, and seek outside opinions on their dickheaded-ness
levels. The Voices of Doubt around you suddenly start to clam up
when you ask them direct questions. The Bullshit Cortex isn't a fair
judge of character. You need to, unfortunately, stare deep into your
soul, and I think this is a good time to go back to your 'shed'.

Remember at the start of this book, when we figured out our
motivation for going on this journey? For me it was my house and

my life in general, but for you maybe it's something else. Maybe you want more money to buy nice clothes for your kid, you want to be able to afford a house so you can have a dog, you want a fancy car so you can drive it slowly past your enemy's house and show them what a success you are.

Whatever it is, there's where you **came from**, where you **want to go**, and **what steps you have to take to get there.**

Hopefully you can still remember that feeling. Remember who you were when you were in your shed. And you should be able to compare **who you were then** to **who you are now.**

By this point, you should be more successful in a number of other ways. Maybe your bank balance has gone up, or your quality of life, or your satisfaction levels.

But has your karma improved? Has your worth as a person? Are you a better person now than you were before? Sure, you might have more material things — clothes, car, bitter enemies — but are you, you as a person, better? Or are you a dickhead?

You have to improve as your life improves or it wasn't worth it.

I like to think I'm still grounded. I still have the same friends and I'm closer to my family now than I was before. I've been able to employ my brother with my production company, buy nice things for my sister's adorable child, provide a nicer life for me and my girlfriend, away from those shagging foxes.

But I still have to do this dickhead inventory ceremony now and again. I go to a quiet room, turn my phone off. Go to a mind palace (or whatever you want to call it, where you stare at a wall for a bit and just think)('thinky castle')('the prison of the intellect') and take stock of the last couple of months. Am I on the right path? Has any success that's come my way changed me? Am I still doing what I'm doing for the right reasons? Does my soul feel full? Am I a dickhead?

And when I'm able to look myself in the mirror and proudly say, 'No I'm not'—

— or, at least, 'Well maybe I am a bit but not that much' —

— then I'm happy. And I hope you will be, too.

EPILOGUE

So you made it, and you're a great success. I'm proud of you, and I'm proud of me, too. I'll look forward to meeting you at Success Club, a secret members-only society that normal people can't Google (so don't try it, now! Google will know that you are not yet a success and block the results! Google is smart!) where we can share a cigar and a glass of fine, expensive brandy. I don't even like brandy. I just drink it because successful people do.

But success isn't the only reason to bullshit your way to #1. Not every idea has to be about a fantastic new entrepreneurial venture.

What I hope you've learned from this book is that practical thinking can get you out of a lot of lows and funks that your brain might put you into.

I hope you've learned that success isn't weighed in material wealth and goods, but success is up here (really would help me out a lot if you can imagine me pointing to my head at this point).

Businesses and ideas that drive money and hype and take you to more successful places are great, sure. But maybe your brain is only able to produce chocolate-flavoured corn flake ideas.

Even if that's the case, you still want to get out of your 'shed'. And you still can. With positive, ordered thinking — taking time to weigh up PROs and CONs, knowing when it's true negativity and when it's just your Bullshit Cortex speaking, listening to friends who are positive as well as negative, knowing your own worth, thinking around every angle of your idea — you can change your whole worldview, and thus, your whole life.

That's what I did. In many ways, my 'shed' was metaphorical as well as physical. I was in a rut, and my shed was a reflection of it.

But **one idea** electrified me out of there and it will happen for you, too.

I have an old adage I like to use whenever I'm actively trying to come up with something new (and, remember, the best ideas often hit you like lightning, but sometimes you're put on the spot and have to think yourself up one to make things happen): **it takes ten bad ideas to have a good one.**

I like to write down all my bad ideas. Chocolate cornflakes. Bunny beauty pageants. Teaching pigs to sit. You've seen them all through this book. **Original ideas are easy to come by, while good ideas are exceedingly rare.**

Having a good idea and having a bad idea takes up the same section of your brain. It's the same muscles moving, just in a different way. Just like doing leg presses at the gym isn't the equivalent of jumping, but when you train enough you can jump higher, so having a lot of bad ideas when it doesn't matter means **you're more likely to have a good one when it does.**

So here's your final toolkit: get a little notepad. Lined, unlined, I don't care. Get a nice pen. Write down ten shitty ideas a day. You can have one now, try it. What if...they built steps to the moon. Cheeto-flavoured cheesecake. What if they painted faces on the front of aeroplanes.

Every morning, write ten ideas down before you do anything. Clear your brain out. And when you're stuck for creativity, go back and read them. Treasure them.

Every bad idea takes you one inch closer to the good idea that might change your life.

That's what Martin Davey, and Georgio Peviani, and selling shells on a beach were to me. I wonder what they might be for you?

Happy bullshitting. See you at the Success Club.

ACKNOWLEDGEMENTS

First I want to acknowledge the Obeah witchcraft which has dominated and shaped every major decision I've ever made in my life: it's a robust and often misunderstood form of spirituality that has become my rock during a tumultuous year of my life. I'd like to thank my family (they know their names), girlfriend (same) and friends (all my friends know their own names). I'd also like to thank Colin the chicken handler, Georgio Peviani and myself. Keep on shittin'.